SIMPLE
TAROT
DECK

Companion Guidebook

Angie Green

The Simple Tarot
www.thesimpletarot.com

TABLE OF CONTENTS

How to Use this Book

This short guidebook is designed to be used with The Simple Tarot Deck. It will act as a short introduction to the tarot card meanings, and contains everything you need to know to get started reading tarot cards with confidence.

This book is divided into three sections.

Section One introduces you to the cards and how to use them in your life.

Section Two gives you a short description of each card with card meanings, interpretations, and actionable advice.

Section Three includes common patterns and symbols you'll find on the cards, which will help you read any tarot deck based on the Waite-Smith tradition.

This guidebook can be used with any tarot deck based on the Rider-Waite-Smith traditional tarot deck, which contains 78 cards divided into the Major Arcana and Minor Arcana.

The Majors contain the first 22 cards (The Fool through The World) and each card represents a major archetype or life lesson.

The Minors describe everyday experiences, problems, and solutions. They are divided into four suits (Cups, Pentacles, Swords, and Wands). Each suit contains 10 numbered cards (Ace through Ten) plus four court cards (Page, Knight, Queen, and King).

For more detailed information for each card, including keywords, reversed meanings, and correspondences, get *Simple Tarot Card Meanings: Learn to Read Tarot Cards* by Angie Green.

HOW TO READ THE CARDS

Tarot has a deep history, but these cards are yours. Use them to help you brainstorm ideas, solve problems, and coach yourself to new opportunities.

There is no right way or wrong way to read the cards. There is only YOUR way.

There are 78 different tarot cards and each card can be interpreted in multiple ways. Trying to memorize the meanings will take too long and doesn't work anyway.

Cheat your way to understanding by learning the patterns and symbols behind the cards. Use this book or any other resource you find helpful, including the tarot cheat sheet found at TheSimpleTarot.com.

You do not need to bless these cards. You don't need to shuffle in a special way. You can flip the cards that are upside-down (reversed) so they are right-side-up. There is no right or wrong way. Do what works for you.

When you have a problem in your life, use the cards to brainstorm new options and new ways of thinking. Break old habits and patterns by pushing your own boundaries.

Ask the cards a question and let them suggest an answer or new way of thinking. Go deeper than just Yes or No, and ask How, Why, and What-next based questions. The cards will tell you a story when read together, so try a tarot spread with multiple cards when you need to go deeper.

If you want to learn the card meanings and internalize their patterns, start integrating the cards into your daily life by pulling one card each day and recording your thoughts. Come back to it the next day to see how that card played out. What did you see? What did you miss?

Persistence beats Resistance. Daily action is far more important than talent, intelligence, or ability. Repetition is key, both for learning the tarot card meanings and for personal growth.

THE CARDS

Like all tarot decks based on the Waite-Smith tradition, The Simple Tarot Deck contains 78 cards divided into the Major Arcana and Minor Arcana.

The Majors contain the first 22 cards (The Fool through The World) and each card represents a major archetype or life lesson.

The Minors describe everyday experiences, problems, and solutions. They are divided into four suits (Cups, Pentacles, Swords, and Wands). Each suit contains 10 numbered cards (Ace through Ten) plus four court cards (Page, Knight, Queen, and King).

Each card can be interpreted in multiple ways. The meanings and ideas in this section will get you started, but for more in-depth information, visit the Tarot Card Meanings section of TheSimpleTarot.com.

THE FOOL

0 - The Fool

When you are wondering what will happen next, The Fool shows up to tell you something awesome (and totally unknown and unexpected) is about to happen. It's here to show you where you need to bring more fun, adventure, and playfulness into your life.

Overall, The Fool is optimistic, self-focused, and blind to reality. In its most positive readings, The Fool is about starting a new adventure with enthusiasm and fresh hope. In a negative sense, it can be read as being stuck in immaturity, self-delusions, and short-term thinking.

THE MAGICIAN

1 - The Magician

The Magician is known as "The Alchemist," the creator who makes something out of nothing. This card is about expressing your unique talents and turning them into something tangible in the world. It is an active, outwardly-focused card and is paired with The High Priestess, which is The Magician's receptive and inwardly-focused magical counterpart.

Although it seems a bit woo-woo, this is a very practical card. The Magician guides you to create an environment, triggers, and routines to regularly and consistently bring yourself to a state of creative flow where you can make your own magic.

THE HIGH PRIESTESS

2 - The High Priestess

There is wisdom within each of us. Wisdom comes from our past mistakes, lessons, and experiences, but it also comes from deeper within us, encoded into our humanity by thousands of years of existence. The High Priestess card represents that deeper understanding.

When you see this card, something - maybe many things - remains hidden. There is a mystery here and it can only be uncovered by trusting your instincts and intuition.

This card is paired with The Magician, the active and outwardly-focused card that precedes it in the Major Arcana.

THE EMPRESS

3 - The Empress

The Empress is the card for fertility and abundance, and for the lusty Earth energy of sensual pleasures. The Empress births new projects in an abundant garden. But gardens take work. Be prepared to plant the seeds, tend your garden, and work for the harvest. She'll provide the abundant harvest, but only with your desire, dedication, work and direction. The work doesn't need to be drudgery (in fact, it shouldn't be!), but The Empress only works when you do.

This is a great card if you're looking to start or grow a creative project. The Empress LOVES creativity and artistic endeavors.

THE EMPEROR

4 - The Emperor

The Emperor is the father-figure of the tarot cards, partnered with the motherly Empress. This card represents active, outwardly-focused energy of vision combined with discipline and perseverance. He's the person you want in your reading, or in your life, when you are looking for practical, logical, and steady guidance. There's nothing wild here. It's all solid ambition, discipline, and hard work.

This card arrives when it's time to take hands-on, practical action toward your ambitious goals. You MUST do the hard work required to see success. Half-measures won't do. You must commit to your dreams, with discipline, passion, and strategy.

THE HIEROPHANT

5 - The Hierophant

The Hierophant tarot card represents conventional society, authority figures, and doing things the "right" way. It can represent a teacher of divine wisdom or it can carry a lesson about your role in society. It's natural to desire the acceptance and approval of the people you love. Being a member of a family, a community, and a society comes with certain (usually unstated) expectations and rules. No matter how you feel about it, everyone has a need for social approval and is concerned with how they fit into their world.

Use The Hierophant to guide you toward a path you are comfortable with, within the system.

THE LOVERS

6 - The Lovers

Everyone loves The Lovers. This is the tarot card for true-love partnerships and long-term happy relationships. But The Lovers is not a card about romantic love only. This card represents a true, soul-level partnership where the personalities or elements are in total, healthy balance. This could be in a friendship, business partnership, or any place where two vibrant forces come together.

You may be faced with a choice between two opposing forces, people, roles, or positions. Something that looks good on paper might not be the right choice. To make the best decision, follow your heart and choose what is best for YOU.

THE CHARIOT

7 - The Chariot

The Chariot vroom-vroom-vrooms into your life with a message of power through focused and deliberate action. This lesson is about taking deliberate action NOW, even though you don't see the full path or even your destination. You can't think, research, or plan your way to greater understanding. Taking action is the only way to learn more about yourself and your world.

The way may not be crystal clear and you may not feel confident, but if you start with the first step, everything else falls into place. You will be able to adjust your course along the way.

STRENGTH

8 - Strength

This card, also known as "The Healer," represents the lessons you learn and the strength you gain when you understand and fully accept all aspects of yourself.

It's like you know, deep in your soul, that you have the inner strength to overcome any obstacle in your path. Yeah, you'll be tested, but you don't even care. You've got this.

There might be lessons about trust and betrayal, friends and enemies, or the facade versus reality. But you have the courage and inner confidence to survive and thrive through them all.

THE HERMIT

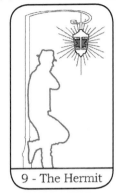

9 - The Hermit

The Hermit is the card of solitude and withdrawal.

When you are faced with a tough situation or difficult decision, The Hermit whispers, "You already have all of the answers you need. You just need to go deep within yourself to find them."

Hone your intuition through deep self-knowledge. Quiet contemplation, meditation, and removal from the stresses and hassles of your daily life will help you strengthen your intuition. When you go within yourself, you will find the solutions you are looking for.

THE WHEEL OF FORTUNE

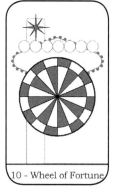

10 - Wheel of Fortune

Usually a good omen, The Wheel of Fortune suggests lucky success and good fortune. There is an element of things changing for the better, so go for it and take your chances. Good luck is usually about being well prepared and standing in the right place at the right time.

There will soon be a major change in your life. This card works quickly. To help your luck along, put yourself out there by asking inspiring and influential people for actionable advice about a single problem you are facing. Take their advice and follow up with them with your results. You'll be making your own luck in no time!

JUSTICE

11 - Justice

If you've been naughty, the Justice card is a tough card to see. This card arrives when things are out of balance and it highlights the consequences of your behavior.

You need to walk your talk. How you earn, spend, save, and invest your money and time represents what you value in the world. It's your vote on what you want to exist.

Align your daily decisions, even little ones like where you choose to buy lunch or how much time you spend making breakfast, with your values and integrity. Your money, time, and energy are powerful tools, so use them wisely.

THE HANGED MAN

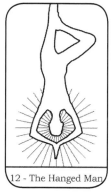

12 - The Hanged Man

The Hanged Man represents the lessons learned when you take responsibility for your actions and then accept their consequences.

You need to release the tight grip you hold on your ideas and the situation at hand. That won't work anymore, so become the agent of change by making a sacrifice to break the old patterns. When you feel betrayed, like a victim, or ashamed of your own actions, look at things from a different point of view.

We can only control ourselves. Everything else we must release and accept with grace.

DEATH

13 - Death

Despite the imagery, this card rarely has anything to do with actual, physical death. Instead, it's a card of rebirth with a message to let go of the past to move on to something better. The Death card indicates involuntary changes and major transformations. Be prepared for the worst, but expect the best eventual outcome.

Like the mythical Phoenix rising from the ashes, the Death card indicates one cycle is ending and another is beginning. There is a major transition happening where you must leave your old life and start something new.

TEMPERANCE

14 - Temperance

The Temperance tarot card seems boring, especially sandwiched between the Death card and The Devil. But this card serves as a reminder to remain patient and go with the flow. You can't ever control a situation, but you can wait it out. You can't ever control other people, but you can be patient as they learn their own mistakes.

These are tough lessons to learn and even tougher to put into practice. Renewal and rejuvenation are coming, so don't go to extremes or force something to happen. Keep your focus on your values and don't let yourself be thrown off track by the influences of others, of your Ego, or of your base emotions.

THE DEVIL

15 - The Devil

The Devil card represents temptation and indulgent sensual pleasures. You know it's bad for you, but it feels so very, very good.

This card is usually seen as a warning against obsessions, compulsions, and addictions. It is so easy to become a slave to the material and physical world. These desires can quickly turn toward greed, exploitation, and oppression.

On the other hand, you may need to start enjoying the pleasures of life. Let yourself become spontaneous and playful, and begin exploring your deepest, naughtiest desires without fear, shame, or excess.

THE TOWER

16 - The Tower

The Tower represents unexpected, unwanted, and unseen change. The Tower shows up when things are about to drastically change in your life.

Things are going to get worse before they get better. The change is ultimately good, but some hard times are about to go down before you get there. You are under attack from forces beyond your control or understanding. There is nothing you can do.

The Tower is necessary for change and growth. Ultimately, there is something wonderful on the other side of this pain, but the only way out of this mess is to go through it.

THE STAR

17 - The Star

The Star tarot card is sometimes called "the fairy godmother" card, because it arrives to let you know everything is going to work out fine. This is very good news, especially after the upheaval of The Tower, which proceeds it. Have faith and believe that things are going to be okay, or even better than okay. They always have been and they always will be.

Sometimes, The Star is about being in the spotlight. If you've ever wanted to see your name in lights, it's time to take center stage. Be authentically you and let your true light shine through.

THE MOON

18 - The Moon

Be on the lookout for unseen problems, deceptions, and haters. You could easily let your imagination and subconscious take you to dark and unfriendly places, so keep your anxiety in check.

Proceed with caution and prudence, but always let your intuition be your guide. This card is a VERY strong call to trust yourself. While The Star is about trusting the Universe, The Moon is about trusting yourself.

Pay attention to what isn't said or what isn't seen. Your imagination and creativity will guide you.

THE SUN

19 - The Sun

The Sun has a clear and positive message about the connection between a fun, positive attitude and good health, happiness, and success. It's time to honor and mark your growth. This is an active card about celebrating how far you've come. You've been working and growing with focus, so take the time to show gratitude with a sense of child-like wonder.

Celebrating and showing gratitude for your success is mandatory. Don't put it off or immediately start striving for something better. When you recognize and acknowledge your accomplishments, you allow even more wonderful things to happen.

JUDGMENT

20 - Judgment

The Judgment card has a big message for you. You can no longer hide or ignore the truths of your life. It's not possible to pretend any more. This card is a huge wakeup call for renewal and transformation.

You see clearly. You know exactly what your passions, desires, and values are. You know your place in the world and how you can best serve.

And with this information, you can't stay stuck. You have no choice but to remove everything that no longer fits with who you are and move into living the life you were meant to live.

THE WORLD

21 - The World

The World is the last card of the Major Arcana. This is a card of closure. You have fulfilled your purpose and goal.

Now it's time to start another one.

Sometimes that means beginning again with The Fool, either learning a new lesson or experiencing the same lesson at a deeper level.

And, sometimes, it means going on an adventure! This is a great card if you are want to take a long trip or relocate to another location. All signs are positive for your new path.

ACE OF CUPS

Ace of Cups

The Ace of Cups represents true love and emotional fulfillment. But unlike a lot of the emotional Cups cards, this one is very active. It's about making things happen.

So, while it may indicate an outpouring of love is coming your way, it could also mean YOU are the one who needs to take a big emotional risk and ask for what you want.

Open your heart to love and be vulnerable. It's the scariest thing of them all, but it's also the only way to get the healthy, fulfilling, and abundant love you desire.

TWO OF CUPS

2 of Cups

Everyone LOVES the Two of Cups. This is the Love Card, after all. But it is about much more than romantic love. It's a very positive card when dealing with any relationship pairing or partnership.

This card strongly indicates romance, attraction, and love. In situations where romance isn't the focus, it can also mean a strong business partnership, friendship, or other relationship between two parties. It's a particularly good card when trying to build a shared understanding or when you are working toward a common goal.

THREE OF CUPS

3 of Cups

The Three of Cups indicates abundance and pleasure as well as celebrations and fun.

But it's not just about celebrating the good times. It's about celebrating the good times with the people who matter most to you. It's a card about community and support.

The Three of Cups is a fantastic card to see when you are feeling alone, stagnant, or unloved. It's telling you to rally the troops, throw a party, and get your groove back on!

FOUR OF CUPS

4 of Cups

The Four of Cups represents what happens when you feel so unfulfilled and bored with your life that you've become blind to the gifts and opportunities sitting right in front of you. Start by asking yourself some tough questions: Are you truly living the life you imagined for yourself? Or have you settled for what was easiest or expected of you?

This is not the time to barrel gung-ho into something new. Instead, take it slow. Spend time quietly contemplating and exploring your options. Make one small step and then re-evaluate. It is your responsibility to understand everything happening in your environment before you make a permanent decision.

FIVE OF CUPS

5 of Cups

The Five of Cups is about loss, regrets, and feeling abandoned. And even more than that, it's about being stuck wallowing in a place where you can't find hope or help.

You need to move through the stages of loss and grief so you can get on with your life. Feel the pain, forgive the people you have lost, forgive yourself, and forge a new life.

It's actually less painful to accept the reality of your situation and move on than it is to live on the dregs of what someone else can't (or won't) give you.

SIX OF CUPS

6 of Cups

The Six of Cups is the card of nostalgia, happy memories, and reunions with people you haven't seen in awhile. It's also associated with the happiness of childhood and golden innocence.

And finally, it's a card that indicates gifts, sensual pleasures (NOT sexual ones), and fun times shared with others. It's a friendly, playful card reminding you to add more silliness and whimsy into your life.

A happy memory may help you solve or address an issue or problem you are facing. Look toward your past for lessons about the present.

SEVEN OF CUPS

7 of Cups

Be careful what you wish for! The Seven of Cups is about fantasy, illusion, and unquenchable desires.

This card shows up when you are living in your daydreams and wishes for the future, believing in your own fantasy in order to escape reality without doing anything to actually change your life.

It's not completely negative, though. It can also indicate a situation where you have too many wonderful choices or where you are in the creative dreaming phase of a new project.

EIGHT OF CUPS

8 of Cups

The Eight of Cups is about successfully moving on from the past. You haven't learned all of the lessons you need to learn, but you are ready to let go of what isn't working and search for the answers. You've realized it's time to abandon what is no longer working for you and you are willing to look for a new way of doing things.

You don't see the full path in front of you, but the moon (which represents your intuition and inner wisdom) is guiding you toward where you need to go. The message of this card is, "It's time to let go of what isn't working and follow your intuition to find what will."

NINE OF CUPS

9 of Cups

The Nine of Cups is about having enough - even a bit more than enough - of all the good things in life. You have emotional resources in reserves.

Your desires WILL be fulfilled. The Universe can be very literal, so be careful and clear when making your requests. Love, creativity, security, good health, and happiness are all yours. You just have to ask with clarity and decisive intention.

The Nine of Cups can sometimes tilt toward over-indulgence and dissatisfaction. Sincere gratitude is the antidote to worry and lack.

TEN OF CUPS

10 of Cups

The Ten of Cups is the card of complete emotional fulfillment. It's an excellent card for relationships, and you can create your own family. Not everyone deserves to be a part of your inner circle, and a genetic connection doesn't guarantee kindness or love. Only you can decide who is worthy of your trust, loyalty, and support.

But once you've created your family, they will become your biggest cheerleaders, your favorite people, your most fun playmates, and your strongest support system. Your family - whatever way you design it - will be at the center of your life and you wouldn't have it any other way.

PAGE OF CUPS

Page of Cups

Like all court cards, the Page of Cups can represent
an actual person in your life. This person is likely to be
younger, creative, sweet, fun-loving, and a bit silly. This card
can also represent a role you need to play in your own life,
or aspects of your personal development you are ready to
focus on. In that situation, this card is telling you to open
your heart and learn to trust your own emotions.

The Page is often a messenger, carrying a lesson.
Information may come from unexpected sources, but don't
discount the message because it comes from an unusual
messenger. Keep an open mind and an open heart, and
look beneath the surface of your experiences.

KNIGHT OF CUPS

Knight of Cups

The Knight of Cups is your Prince (or Princess) Charming, your knight in shining armor, and your ultimate lover. THIS is the card about romance, desire, and loveable charm.

Like all of the court cards, this Knight usually represents an actual person in your life. Lucky you! If not someone in your life, the Knight of Cups could be telling you to step up, romantically speaking.

Bring more of this knight's energy into your own life, first by seducing yourself and then by turning that energy toward your heart's desire.

QUEEN OF CUPS

Queen of Cups

The Queen of Cups is the ruler of your inner emotions. This queen wants you to love completely, without giving up too much of yourself. This isn't a card about self-denial or codependent love. If you trust yourself to protect your boundaries, you will have nothing to fear by loving deeply, selflessly, and with joy.

This card, like all of the court cards, often represents an actual person in your life. This will be someone (male or female) who is deeply loving, sensitive, and compassionate. The Queen of Cups can also represent a role you are ready to play in your own life or a message you need to hear.

KING OF CUPS

King of Cups

The King of Cups is the master of loyalty, commitment, and love. He's a great guide and counselor who oversees his domain with kindness, tolerance, and dependability.

Like all of the court cards, the King of Cups usually stands for an actual person in your life. In this case, it would be a loving and generous person (male or female) who is a wonderful life-partner and parent or who has the potential to be one, given the right circumstances. This card can also represent a role you are ready to play in your own life. Model the King of Cups' dependability, loyalty, and trust by being dependable, loyal, and trustworthy yourself.

ACE OF PENTACLES

Ace of Pentacles

The Ace of Pentacles is about the beginning of a new financial quest or creative endeavor. It represents the "seed money" you need to grow your future. If you are questioning your path, you are in the right place and you have a great idea. Pursue it. Someone will give you the resources you need or you will find yourself in a situation where the resources appear, almost as if they are coming out of thin air.

This is an active card. You must do the work. Change won't happen overnight, but it is guaranteed to happen if you keep taking daily action toward your goals without quitting. Success is 100% within your power and control.

TWO OF PENTACLES

2 of Pentacles

The Two of Pentacles is about maintaining balance and keeping all of your balls in the air. You are balancing resources (such as time or money) or you need to make a decision between two things.

Whatever your situation, you will have to make a decision and take action on it. You can't keep juggling options, researching possibilities, and stalling your future forever. Keeping your options open will only leave you with options, not commitment or forward motion.

THREE OF PENTACLES

3 of Pentacles

The Three of Pentacles is about teamwork, collaboration, and building great things together with others. It takes practice to learn any skill. This is the time to learn your craft. Your skill and attention to detail will allow you make your own luck and you will become an overnight success only after years of dedicated and deliberate practice.

But it's not only about you. No one gets to the top of their game alone. You will be creatively building your career in collaboration with others. Partner with peers in your industry as well as people outside of your field of focus. By expanding your network and your sources of inspiration, you will grow faster and farther toward your dreams.

FOUR OF PENTACLES

4 of Pentacles

The Four of Pentacles is about gathering, investing, and sharing what you have. Looking on the bright side, this card is about investing in yourself to create a solid foundation. You are feeling extremely security-conscious. You want to take care of yourself and build a future for the people you love.

On the other side of the coin, it's about hoarding and always wanting more. This results in the Four of Pentacles being a greedy miser who takes but never gives. Money, like all energy, needs to move. Share what you can with the people who need it and you'll soon see more coming your way.

FIVE OF PENTACLES

5 of Pentacles

The Five of Pentacles is one of the scariest and most unwanted cards of the deck. No one likes to think about illness, money problems, or being out in the cold without help. Yet, we all have trying times in our lives. This card is a warning sign to remind us that we must prepare for when the tough times come again.

It's time to build up and protect your reserves, take care of yourself, and ask for help. You don't need to be completely independent and self-sufficient. Learn the power and security of interdependence and connection and you'll be able to trust your safety net will always be there.

SIX OF PENTACLES

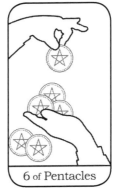

6 of Pentacles

The Six of Pentacles wants you to share your time, resources, and skills so others can prosper. In doing so, you'll benefit, too. This card can mean financial success, a raise, or a bonus is headed your way. But generosity goes both ways. Give others the gift of giving to you by receiving with grace. Be open to taking what is offered and graciously accepting the gifts given to you.

If you are needing help, ask for it. And if you have extra resources (of time, money, energy, knowledge, etc.), then share what you have with others. You'll both benefit and you'll likely learn something new along the way.

SEVEN OF PENTACLES

7 of Pentacles

The Seven of Pentacles is about doing the work, not about the finished project. This card represents the long, hard slog of any large challenge. Success will eventually come, but don't focus on the results. Enjoy the process and keep doing the work. It will soon pay off.

This card can also represent job dissatisfaction or a sabbatical from work. Before you make any big decisions, reevaluate your goals, desires, and dreams. Be patient in your current position for things to change. It may be time to move on.

EIGHT OF PENTACLES

8 of Pentacles

The Eight of Pentacles is about becoming a master of your craft. When you've found the right profession, sometimes work feels like play. You can get so lost in the flow of what you're doing that hours pass without you realizing it.

Everyone knows you are a master at what you do. You have the history (and the body of work behind you) to prove it.

Keep learning and perfecting your skills. Even though you have reached or on the path to expert status and could rest on your laurels, you'll enjoy your work more if you focus on continued improvement.

NINE OF PENTACLES

9 of Pentacles

This is the card for individual prosperity and personal luxury. This isn't the luxury of having a new convertible every year, or living on a yacht without ever having to do another day of work in your life. You aren't resting on your laurels.

Instead, you're enjoying them. True luxury means different things to different people, and this card is about recognizing and honoring what your true definition of luxury is.

Find your simplicity and independence by acknowledging and living this experience of ultimate personal satisfaction.

TEN OF PENTACLES

10 of Pentacles

The Ten of Pentacles indicates a solid future with happiness, safety, and long-term security. Your assets and resources will grow into a gift for the next generation. As dreary as it may sound, creating a will and an estate plan is an act of generosity, hope, and commitment. Create a plan today for how your money, property, and assets will be directed once you are gone.

You are leaving a legacy with your choices and actions. Others in your family, especially children, are watching how you treat yourself and take care of your own needs. Every choice you make is a lesson for them, so choose carefully and well.

PAGE OF PENTACLES

Page of Pentacles

This card, like all of the court cards, often refers to a real person in your life or a role you play. The Page of Pentacles specifically indicates a young student or someone who studies every angle of a decision before they make their choice. The Page is someone who searches for more efficient and effective ways of doing things. He or she sticks to the problem until it is solved and completes every project until the end.

It can also be about research, learning, or industrious effort. It teaches you how to master your skills, talents, and creativity and helps you put your abilities to work.

KNIGHT OF PENTACLES

Knight of Pentacles

Like all of the court cards, the Knight of Pentacles can represent an actual person in your life, a role you play (or need to play), or a message you are ready to hear.

If it's an actual person, the card specifically represents someone hard-working, patient and methodical. This person may love nature and take good care of their body, but probably is uncomfortable with strong emotions.

If this card doesn't represent an actual person, the lessons are about teaching yourself (or others) how to work hard and complete projects. It's not very exciting, but it is effective!

QUEEN OF PENTACLES

Queen of Pentacles

The Queen of Pentacles has the best garden of all of the queens, where everything is constantly in bloom. She has created abundance through daily discipline and a healthy approach to life. She loves nature and is a resourceful manager of everything in her domain.

Like all of the court cards, this card may represent an actual person in your life, specifically a nurturing person (male or female) who has a loving, gentle, and wise demeanor. If not someone in your life, it may represent a role you are currently playing or are ready to play.

KING OF PENTACLES

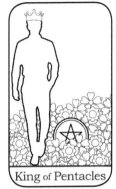

King of Pentacles

The King of Pentacles is the master of material and worldly success, and represents the qualities of hard work, practicality, generosity, and common sense. Like all of the court cards, this card may indicate an actual man or woman in your life, a role you play (or need to play), or a message you are ready to hear.

Become this King by paying attention to every detail, using common sense, and doing the work you find most challenging. Always take the high road, hold yourself and others to high standards, and maintain strong boundaries as you give energy and time toward creating a better world.

ACE OF SWORDS

Ace of Swords

The Ace of Swords cuts through to the truth. Using this sword, you can force a situation to be dealt with quickly.

This is not a card of inner wisdom, research, thought, or inaction. The Ace of Swords helps you take charge of a situation. When you combine new ideas with swift action, you'll see success.

A sword can cut both ways, so this card can indicate the start of a new idea or challenge, or it may mean the start of a conflict or problem.

TWO OF SWORDS

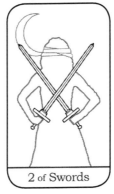

2 of Swords

The Two of Swords is for when you feel torn between two options or are balancing two opposing forces in your life. A decision needs to be made (and you will likely make the right one), but you may want to compromise or find a different way from your normal choices.

Do not rely on logic or your intellect too much. Use your intuition to make the best decision.

This is NOT the time for bold action. You must go within to find the balance and inner wisdom you need. There is no deadline for this decision, but you will feel relief once it is made.

THREE OF SWORDS

3 of Swords

The Three of Swords is about heartbreak and loss. There's not any way to avoid sorrow in life, unfortunately.

Every relationship has down periods, where quarrels and miscommunication seem to happen more often than joy, adventure, and love. But whatever happens, you will come out of it stronger and with more clarity about yourself, your needs, and your values. Just because this period is hard doesn't mean it's bad.

The only way out of the pain is through it. You will have to feel it and you can't run away from it. But you can (and will) heal from this, so don't be afraid of your feelings.

FOUR OF SWORDS

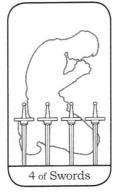

4 of Swords

The Four of Swords is your call to retreat into yourself for rest, meditation, and recovery. This is THE card for seclusion and solitude. It is no surprise it follows the Three of Swords (the card for heartbreak). When you've felt deep loss, you need time to recover and heal.

Focus on your own self-care, especially on building your inner world. This doesn't have to be a month-long retreat to a cabin in the woods (although that's a wonderful idea if you can do it). Small daily actions, like meditating, journaling, or a media fast will give you the time and mental space to retreat from the world.

FIVE OF SWORDS

5 of Swords

The Five of Swords shows someone (you?) spoiling for a fight. You're in the war zone and this conflict can't be avoided.

Unfortunately, this conflict is likely to be unequal, unfair, or abusive. You do have a choice, though. You can fight this unfair fight or you can learn from the situation, grow, and move on.

Of course, the better option is to learn from this situation. Fighting this battle will likely end in defeat. Even if you do somehow come out on top, the victory will be hollow and you'll lose much more than you hoped to gain.

Six of Swords

6 of Swords

When you are ready to leave your sorrows behind and start a new life, the Six of Swords is for you. You must look at things as they actually are, not as you wish them to be. Accept the reality of the situation, no matter how painful it is to admit the truth.

Once you move on, the struggle will be over. The pain will be in your past. You are ready for something new, even though you don't know what the future holds.

This a very hopeful card. Once you take action to move toward your new future, you will have smooth sailing and things will change with ease.

SEVEN OF SWORDS

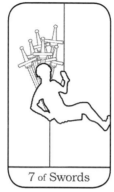

7 of Swords

The Seven of Swords tarot card is about betrayal through trickery and dishonesty. Someone is being sneaky or is lying to you (or about you).

When you have someone gossiping about you, copying you, or hating on you in some way, it's rooted in jealousy. As much as their words and behaviors hurt, their judgmental and critical behavior actually says more about their wounds than it does about your choices.

If YOU are the jerk who is gossiping, lying, or stealing, be prepared to have the truth come to light quickly. You will have to pay for the pain you've caused.

EIGHT OF SWORDS

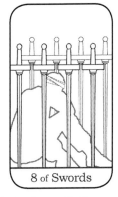

8 of Swords

The Eight of Swords is about feeling trapped and helpless. You are either trapped by fear or by your own unhelpful actions. While there may be some interference from outside forces, it is likely ALL of your current problems are self-imposed.

You have been hijacked by your limiting beliefs. Although the beliefs feel real, they are holding you back. The only way to get out of this situation is to take off your blindfold and see the reality of the situation. What you believe is not true. You must change your beliefs, which will allow you to change your thoughts, words, actions, and choices. Change must happen from the inside first.

NINE OF SWORDS

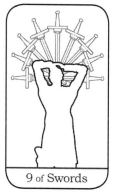

9 of Swords

Everyone feels the grief of the Nine of Swords at some time in their life, but most of us want to move past it as quickly as we can.

Worrying ruins the present and doesn't help the future. The anxiety, unhappiness, and emotional pain of your (physical or mental) situation is making things worse. Stress leads to sleeplessness and isolation, which leads to anxiety, illness, and depression.

You are too far down the rabbit hole to claw your way out on your own. Stop making things so difficult for yourself. Ask for help.

TEN OF SWORDS

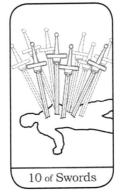

10 of Swords

The Ten of Swords is the card for betrayal and hitting rock bottom, either due to your own actions or the actions of your enemies. Although the general meaning of this card is brutal, it also carries a message that the past is OVER. It no longer holds you and you are free to move in any new direction you choose. That's a freeing and positive thought!

You're in the muck right now, though. There is a sense of total loss and defeat and you are at the absolute bottom. This is a painful and unwanted ending, but you can't deny the situation any longer. What is done is DONE. Your only option is to accept this fact and move on.

PAGE OF SWORDS

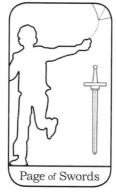

Page of Swords

The Page of Swords, like all the court cards, can be interpreted as an actual person, as a role you play, or as a message. If it is an actual person in your life, it will be a stubborn, curious, talkative person with youthful energy who is constantly learning, but this isn't only book-knowledge. This Page is eager to put information into action. Sometimes that eager energy means the Page acts without a plan or road map. This reckless action rarely brings positive results.

If you are struggling, you can't wish for change. You must create a plan and then take step-by-step daily action to improve your situation.

KNIGHT OF SWORDS

Knight of Swords

The Knight of Swords can represent a soldier, a fearless crusader, or any youthful person who enters your life quickly to stir it up. Whoever this Knight is, it is someone who charges forward and acts quickly. They HATE to be held back. He or she is always on the move and is often seen as being rash and impulsive.

He's generally not actually rash or impulsive, however. He just thinks faster than the rest of us!

This Knight's message is to create your own path. Don't spend the time searching for the easiest or most common way. Make your own way.

QUEEN OF SWORDS

Queen of Swords

The Queen of Swords tarot card, like all court cards, often represents an actual person in your life. It can also mean a role you are playing or need to play. If this is an actual person, it will be a man or woman who is a fierce protector. This Queen is logical, intellectual, and never acts rashly. You may not like her. In fact, many people think she's stuck-up, but she is always objective and fair. Her heart is in the right place. This woman calls things as they are and is fearless critic of ignorance, unfairness, and injustice. If you are faced with a problem at work, you already know the answer. Call things as they are and take action to correct anything unfair or unjust. Think clearly and then act decisively.

KING OF SWORDS

King of Swords

The King of Swords is as good with words as he is with thought and action. This is the type of person who will carefully think through a decision and be intentional in their actions. They clearly visualize what they want, need, and desire, and then take immediate and decisive action to get it. If this card is representing an actual person in your life, look for a person (male or female) who is forceful, decisive, and blunt.

If this card represents a role you play in your life, you must get your head, heart, and actions in alignment. You have the power to make great choices, but don't rush.

ACE OF WANDS

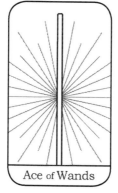

Ace of Wands

The Ace of Wands tarot card is definitely a good omen. It blazes with the urge to create. It could be a new career, a new baby, a new relationship, or a new direction in your life. This card thrusts quickly with a desire to bring something new into being. It's a lusty and action-oriented card.

If there has been a passion project you've been putting on the back burner, this is the time to pursue it. Fit it around the edges of your daily routine if you must, and keep the project quiet if you don't think you'll have support. But once the project gets going, it will catch fire on its own and blaze into success.

TWO OF WANDS

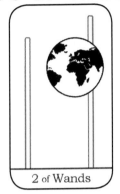

2 of Wands

The Two of Wands is about waiting, planning, and wise decision making. It's a positive card about setting strong intentions and expectations.

You have more than one option, so start doing research, making plans, and creating the road map to lead you into the future.

Decisive action will be needed to realize your goals, so prepare yourself. You are ready to make a decision and choose a future path. No more waffling or waiting or hoping things will get better. If you want things to change - YOU must change. Start by making a solid plan.

THREE OF WANDS

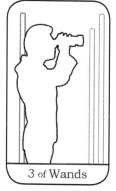

3 of Wands

While the Two of Wands is about the planning and decisions before you take action, the Three of Wands represents the waiting period after action has been taken. It's also a card about collaboration and teamwork, especially in business.

If you are looking for a new opportunity, you must do the work to make things happen. Maintain constant focus and stay the course until the project comes to completion. Any new venture or major expansion involving other people is a good idea. Do the work, think big, pull your weight, and stay positive. Be patient, but your actions will show great results.

FOUR OF WANDS

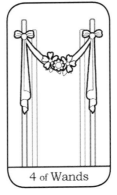

4 of Wands

The Four of Wands is a celebration of love, friendship, and family. This is also the card for reunions, homecomings, celebrations, and parties with friends. Things in your life are all starting to come together and you have built a strong foundation. There is the potential for something even better, but for now celebrate all you have.

The Four of Wands wants you to celebrate where you are, right now. Throw a party, host a potluck, or grill at the park and invite the people who are key to your support network. Tell them your plans and ask for their support. They want to see you succeed, so share your appreciation and enthusiasm with the people who love you most.

FIVE OF WANDS

5 of Wands

The Five of Wands is about the positive challenges you face when you are in conflict or competition with others.

While conflict, rivalry, and strife seem like negative things, they are opportunities for growth. You're going to have to suit up and fight. There's no hiding any more. It is time to commit to reaching your goals at a level that scares you. This means changing your daily routines, beliefs, and habits quickly so you can work with absolute focus and clarity. There is no more room for daydreams and wishes. You need to Do The Work. There are NO exceptions or excuses.

SIX OF WANDS

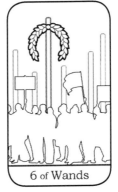

6 of Wands

You have overcome your challenges and are hearing the applause and respect you've earned from your triumph. You are the leader and you are on the right path. The Six of Wands represents the victories and recognition you've gained through your hard work, commitment, and leadership.

People are watching you and are inspired by what you are doing (even if you don't realize it). Your actions matter and your opportunities are spreading far outside your sphere of influence. Continue doing the work that brought you to this point. But for a moment you can take a deep breath and celebrate your position. You've earned it.

SEVEN OF WANDS

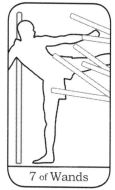

7 of Wands

When you are being tested, the Seven of Wands tells you to stand your ground. You must defend yourself against the bullies, energy vampires, and "helpful" people who think they know what is best for you.

They know nothing. Only YOU know what is best for you. You must stand up for yourself and defend what is most important to you.

Your steadfastness will pay off. Don't compromise or settle for less than what you need and desire. You have to go against the crowd and blaze your own defiant path. Do not let anyone stand in your way.

EIGHT OF WANDS

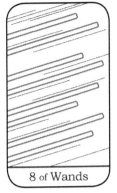

8 of Wands

The Eight of Wands represents important news flying through the air toward you. It can also mean something is quickly changing in your life.

This is a time for excitement and action, so don't hold back. If you meet someone new, be prepared for a whirlwind romance. Cupid's arrows are flying!

When the news arrives (whatever it relates to), you will have to move quickly. The only thing guaranteed is rapid change, so make yourself as prepared as you can be for ALL possible outcomes.

NINE OF WANDS

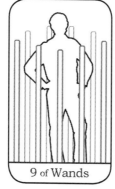

9 of Wands

The Nine of Wands is the card for courage and persistence in the face of challenges. When you're feeling defensive and hurt, it reminds you that you can handle anything if you summon your final reserves and stand for what you believe in. This card can be a warning to watch your back. Without being paranoid, create strong boundaries and defenses to protect the things you've built. Protect the work you do and treat all your output and assets as valuable. Make things as easy for yourself as possible by investing in quality tools, supportive friendships, and professional help. You're worth it and those investments will make a difference in your success.

TEN OF WANDS

10 of Wands

When you are burdened by too many responsibilities and commitments, the Ten of Wands reminds you to shrug off your load and put your own needs first. There is too much stress in your life and too much is landing on your shoulders. Instead of success, all of your hard work is leading toward exhaustion and burnout. You can't go on like this. Learn to say no. And say it loudly and often.

While it may seem like more work in the short-term to delegate and train others, it is necessary. You don't have the option to avoid it any longer. You MUST remove some of the workload or you will damage your company, your career, your relationships, and your health.

PAGE OF WANDS

Page of Wands

The Page of Wands usually represents a fiery, active, creative young person in your life. This is likely to be someone enthusiastic, loyal, rebellious and full of life. If not an actual person, this card can also represent a new creative project, idea, adventure, career path or course of study. Follow your spark and keep an open mind about where it leads you. You are at the beginnings of a new adventure. It will (eventually) require a lot of work, faith, and commitment, but for right now, it's all fun, joy, and play. Follow the threads of what you love and keep moving toward the activities you enjoy. Your heart knows where you belong.

KNIGHT OF WANDS

Knight of Wands

This card, like all the court cards, can represent someone in your life, a role you play, or a message you are ready to hear. If this is an actual person in your life, the Knight of Wands will represent a person (male or female) who is lusty, passionate, and free-spirited. Despite this crusader's free-spirit, this is not someone who is playful or carefree. The Knight of Wands has got a sense of purpose and a very strong will.

If you've been planning, researching, and thinking about something, NOW is the time to take action on it. No more maybes. This is definitely it! Don't wait for everything to be perfect before you act.

QUEEN OF WANDS

Queen of Wands

The Queen of Wands is self-assured with lots of personal magnetism. She has explored and mastered the dark places of her soul and has come out transformed. If this Queen represents someone in your life, it will be a man or woman who easily balances a boundless creative energy with such radiant self-assurance that you can't help but be drawn in by their enthusiasm and commitment.

When this card represents a role you must play or a message you are ready to hear, the Queen of Wands wants YOU to go for your own dreams and will help you commit big-time to your passion and desires.

KING OF WANDS

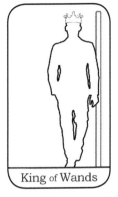

King of Wands

This King's got swagger and knows when to use it. Like all court cards, this card can represent an actual person in your life, a role you need to play, or a message you are ready to hear. If it's a real person, it is someone (male or female) who radiates power. The King of Wands represents a self-starter with charisma, kindness, and creativity. This person will be intense, powerful, and intimidating.

This King commands you to see your own power. He is the master of his own life and knows everything happening to him has been caused by his thoughts, words, and actions. EVERYTHING. He wants you to learn the same.

THE SUITS & THE ELEMENTS

It is easier to understand the cards when you know the underlying patterns and symbols.

The Minor Arcana are divided into the four suits of the Cups, Pentacles, Swords, and Wands. Each suit represents a specific area of your life and is paired with an element of Air, Earth, Fire, or Water.

When you understand the suits and elements, you can combine them with the card numbers or people to get the card's meaning.

For example, the previous card, the King of Wands, is a passionate master of power and creativity.

King = a master of his domain
Wands = passion & personality
Fire = intensity

CUP

Cups are used when we toast in celebration, connect over meals, and drown our sorrows. The cards of the Cups suit represent your relationships and emotional connections.

They have to do with love, friendship, connection, and affairs of the heart.

A person ruled by Cups (or the Water element) will be creative, empathetic, nurturing, intuitive, and caring.

If this energy is taken too far, it will become needy, overly sensitive, easily hurt, and demanding of attentional and emotional validation.

WATER

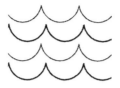

The Water element is represented by the Cups suit.

It is often shown on cards with a strong emotional element, such as the Six of Swords or the Three of Swords (as rain).

Water is also found on the Temperance card and The Star, where it is combined with Earth to represent harmony.

PENTACLE

Pentacles look like coins. The cards of the Pentacles suit represent the physical world, including money, property, worldly possessions, the home, a career, or our physical bodies.

A person ruled by the Pentacles (or the Earth element) will be hard-working, practical, loyal, and stable.

If this energy is taken too far, it can become shallow, petty, dull, boring, or miserly. They make great project managers, but often lose track of the forest because they are too busy counting and cataloging tree leaves.

EARTH

The Earth element is represented by the suit of Pentacles. In tarot, it is often depicted as an abundant garden.

It is often shown on cards with a strong practical or physical element, such as The Magician or The Empress.

SWORD

The 14 cards of the Swords suit represent the intellect, including logical thought and communication.

A sword can cut both ways, and many of the cards in the Swords suit are tough lessons to learn. The swords will cut through confusion, lies, and limiting beliefs. They can be used to attack, and they will allow you to defend your most cherished ideals.

A person ruled by the Swords (or the Air element) will be dynamic, witty, intelligent, and action-oriented.

If this energy is taken too far, it can become cold-hearted, distant, or cruel. They are excellent at solving problems and making plans, but their sharp tongue and cutting words can ruin relationships.

AIR

The Air element is represented by the Swords suit. In tarot, it is often depicted by birds in flight, moving clouds, butterflies, or other beings with wings.

It is often shown on cards with a strong intellectual or logical element, such as the Eight of Wands, the Four of Cups, the Justice card, and The Emperor.

WAND

The 14 cards of the Wands suit represent the burning passions of your personality and spirit. These cards are about creativity, inspiration, ambition, dreams, and goals.

A person ruled by the Wands (or the Fire element) will be driven, passionate, optimistic, energetic, and creative. If this energy is taken too far, it can become self-centered, overly dramatic, rash, or immature. While they may be extremely charismatic and energetic, they sometimes hog the limelight and let their temper blaze into an inferno.

FIRE

The Fire element is represented by the Wands suit. In tarot, it is often depicted by a desert or blazing sun.

It is often shown on cards with a strong element of energy or passion, such as the four Aces and The Sun.

THE NUMBERS

The numbered cards are organized in patterns. Use these patterns, combined with the suits and elements, to read and remember the cards.

For quick reference:

> One = New Beginnings
> Two = Pairings & Choices
> Three = Creating & Connecting
> Four = Stability & Security
> Five = Instability & Crisis
> Six = Community & the New Normal
> Seven = Reflection & Assessment
> Eight = Speed & Power
> Nine = Independence & Solitude
> Ten = Completion

THE ONES

1

The Ones represent fresh starts and new beginnings. Things happen quickly, so you will need to take quick action.

Ace + Cups = new love.

Ace + Pentacles = new job or new investments.

Ace + Swords = new challenges or problems.

Ace + Wands = new ideas or new projects.

The Magician = powerful new creation.

THE TWOS

2

The Twos are about balancing options and making choices. They have to do with pairings, tension, and decisions.

Two + Cups = a strong partnership.

Two + Pentacles = balancing resources.

Two + Swords = a decision is needed.

Two + Wands = pre-project planning & decision-making.

The High Priestess = hidden insights & secrets.

The Threes

3

The Threes represent relationships and connecting with others.

Three + Cups = fun times with friends.

Three + Pentacles = apprenticeship & collaboration.

Three + Swords = heartbreak (the opposite of connection).

Three + Wands = mid-project waiting & teamwork.

The Empress = abundant fertility & creation.

THE FOURS

4

The Fours represent stability, security, and things that don't move. Think of a foundation with four solid corners.

Four + Cups = stagnant stuckness.

Four + Pentacles = seeking security.

Four + Swords = rest & recovery.

Four + Wands = marking life's big moments.

The Emperor = solid & stable discipline.

THE FIVES

5

The Fives are mid-point between the Aces and the Tens, when things turn nasty. They represent instability, isolation, conflict, crisis, and loss.

Five + Cups = focusing on the worst.

Five + Pentacles = physical and financial loss.

Five + Swords = bullies & violence.

Five + Wands = competition & rivalry.

The Hierophant = conformity to the masses.

THE SIXES

6

The Sixes represent the new normal after the chaos and lessons of the Fives. They are about problem-solving in community with others.

Six + Cups = nostalgia & fond memories.

Six + Pentacles = generosity.

Six + Swords = moving on from the past.

Six + Wands = recognition & acclaim.

The Lovers = strong partnerships.

THE SEVENS

7

The Sevens represent reflection and assessment. They act as a warning against those times when you try to justify your actions.

Seven + Cups = wishful thinking & temptations.

Seven + Pentacles = impatience & lethargy.

Seven + Swords = trickery & cutting corners.

Seven + Wands = defending your boundaries & fighting back.

The Chariot = ambitious action forward.

THE EIGHTS

8

The Eights represent movement, speed, and personal power.

Eight + Cups = moving on to find something better.

Eight + Pentacles = mastery of your craft.

Eight + Swords = feeling trapped (the opposite of movement).

Eight + Wands = quickly arriving options & change.

Strength = unconditional personal regard.

THE NINES

9

The Nines represent solitude and independence. They are the personal insights and individual experience you find when you are alone.

Nine + Cups = self-satisfaction.

Nine + Pentacles = individual abundance & luxury.

Nine + Swords = anxiety & nightmares.

Nine + Wands = honoring your boundaries.

The Hermit = insight & understanding.

THE TENS

10

The Tens represent completion and success.

Ten + Cups = family contentment.

Ten + Pentacles = legacy & inheritance.

Ten + Swords = hitting rock bottom (the opposite of success).

Ten + Wands = over-burdened (the opposite of completion).

The Wheel of Fortune = good fortune & luck.

THE PEOPLE (THE COURT CARDS)

The Court Cards usually represent specific people in your life. Your boss might be the King of Wands and your neighbor might be the Queen of Cups. The sex or gender of the person is irrelevant. Knights can be women and Queens can be men.

These pairings are dependent on the situation. Someone might be the King of Wands in their professional life, but the Page of Cups when it comes to romance.

There is usually one Court Card that represents you in any situation.

If you can't pair a Court Card with a specific person in your life, then interpret the card as if it represents a role you need to play or a message you need to hear.

THE PAGES

The Pages are about fresh starts, new lessons, and study.
Their energy is receptive and open-hearted.

They are often young, young-at-heart, or inexperienced
with the situation at hand. If the Page is someone in your
life, it will be someone (man, woman, or child) just starting
to explore the lessons they need to know.

Pages need your support and guidance. They offer loyalty,
enthusiasm, and new ideas.

Page + Cups = learning how to connect with others and
have healthy relationships.

Page + Pentacles = learning how to build resources and
take care of what they have.

Page + Swords = learning how to think clearly and
communicate with authenticity.

Page + Wands = learning how to trust and use their own
power.

THE KNIGHTS

The Knights are about change, challenge, and transformation. Each Knight is in the middle of their quest, adventuring on a Hero's Journey containing obstacles and tests designed specifically for their own personal growth and self-transformation. Their energy is active and energetic, but may be hard to control. If the Knight is someone in your life, it will be a woman or man who is striving with single-minded focus. It may appear that they are going after the Holy Grail of adventure, love, or success, but they are really searching for self-knowledge, discovery, and growth. Knights need you to give them direction and a goal. They offer passion and action toward wherever they (or you) direct their energy.

Knight + Cups = striving for the perfect romance.

Knight + Pentacles = striving for financial or career success.

Knight + Swords = striving for quick actions and change.

Knight + Wands = striving for creative adventures.

THE QUEENS

Queens have faced their own dark side and have come out stronger. Their energy is receptive, compassionate, and intuitive. They are busy and involved, but want to help you. Personal connections are vital.

If the Queen is someone in your life, it will be a woman or man who works their magic behind the scenes. They will use surprising levels of strength to protect, nurture, and defend what they love. They are far more complex than they seem.

Queens need your loyalty, discretion, and authenticity. They offer connections, wisdom, and mentorship.

Queen + Cups = a wise protector of kindness.

Queen + Pentacles = a wise protector of resources.

Queen + Swords = a wise protector of justice.

Queen + Wands = a wise protector of passions and goals.

THE KINGS

Kings are masters of their domain. They are leaders who have proven themselves on the battlefield of life. Their energy is active, assertive, and commanding.

If the King is someone in your life, it will be a man or woman who is at the top of their game. They make decisive and final decisions, delegate everything but their responsibility, and will directly affect the outcome of your situation.

Kings are sometimes inaccessible. They need your understanding and respect about the many demands on their time and energy. They offer solutions, connections, and answers.

King + Cups = a master of relationships and connection.

King + Pentacles = a master of material success.

King + Swords = a master of rational decision-making.

King + Wands = a master of creativity and power.

THE SYMBOLS

In the Waite-Smith tarot tradition, symbols repeat across the cards.

Like the patterns found in the suits, elements, numbers, and people of the court cards, these symbols can help you remember and read the cards.

.

WATER AND EARTH TOGETHER

Water and Earth together represent harmony.

This symbolic representation is found on the Temperance card and The Star.

MOUNTAIN

A mountain used as a symbol is found on The Hermit and the Eight of Cups.

It represents retreating from the world as you create your own path.

CROWN

The crown symbol represents mastery.

It is found on all of the Queen and King court cards as well as The Empress, The Emperor, and The Tower.

ROSE

The rose used as a symbol is found on The Fool, The Magician, the Death card, and many others.

It represents purity (especially when white) and rebirth.

MOON

The moon represents the intuition and subconscious.

It is used as a symbol on The High Priestess, the Two of Swords, and the Eight of Cups.

SUN

The sun represents optimistic positivity and warmth.

The symbol is found on The Sun, the four Aces, and other cards, including many of the fiery Wands.

SUNFLOWER

The sunflower is found on The Sun and the Queen of Wands.

As a symbol, it represents vitality.

CANDLE OR LANTERN

A candle or lantern is found on The Magician, The Hermit, and The World.

It represents illumination and knowledge.

DOG

Dogs are found on The Fool, The Moon, and the Ten of Pentacles.

On The Fool and the Ten of Pentacles, they represent faithful companions.

On The Moon, the domesticated dog represents dreams and the feral dog represents fears.

Other pets include the bunny on the Queen of Pentacles, representing abundance and domesticity, and the black cat on the Queen of Wands, representing her shadow side.

Laurel Wreath

The laurel wreath is the symbol for victory and success.

It is found on The World, the Seven of Cups, and the Six of Wands.

BALANCED SCALES

The balanced scales are found on the Justice card and the Six of Pentacles.

They represent things being in balance.

INFINITY

The infinity symbol (called a lemniscate) is found on The Magician, the Strength card, and the Two of Pentacles.

It represents eternity and the endless nature of energy, which can't be created or destroyed.

ABOUT THE SIMPLE TAROT

Thanks for reading! I hope you found this book useful.

My name is Angie Green and I've created The Simple Tarot website and resources to make learning (and using) tarot cards simple and easy for anyone who is interested in finding creative solutions for life's little problems.

If you've enjoyed this book, please leave a review wherever you bought it. Reviews really matter, both for other tarot lovers and to share your ideas for improvements with the author. I'd love to hear your thoughts about this book & The Simple Tarot.

For more tarot goodies, visit TheSimpleTarot.com for daily tarot-scopes, useful tarot spreads, a free printable Tarot Cheat Sheet, and The Simple Tarot Deck.

72493853R10075

Made in the
USA
Middletown, DE